I0154237

Henry Van Boynton

Was General Thomas slow at Nashville?

Henry Van Boynton

Was General Thomas slow at Nashville?

ISBN/EAN: 9783337395780

Printed in Europe, USA, Canada, Australia, Japan

Cover: Foto ©ninafisch / pixelio.de

More available books at **www.hansebooks.com**

WAS GENERAL THOMAS
SLOW AT NASHVILLE?

WITH A DESCRIPTION OF

*The Greatest Cavalry Movement
of the War*

AND

GENERAL JAMES H. WILSON'S CAVALRY OPERATIONS
IN TENNESSEE, ALABAMA, AND GEORGIA

BY

HENRY V. BOYNTON

*Brevet Brig. Gen. U. S. V.; Historian Chickamauga
and Chattanooga National Park Commission*

———

NEW YORK

FRANCIS P. HARPER

1896

PREFACE.

A RECENT revival of the venerable charge that General George H. Thomas was slow at Nashville led to the publication, in the New York *Sun* of August 9, 1896, of the article which is here reproduced by the permission of that journal. A few brief additions have been made to the original text.

It seemed the more important to some of the veterans of the Army of the Cumberland that this charge in its renewed form should be met, because it was put forth with a show of official authority which would naturally give it weight with readers who were not familiar with the war records.

The discussion of the subject also afforded an opportunity to present, though in very concise form, the outlines of those magnificent cavalry operations under General James H. Wilson in the battle of Nashville, and in his subsequent independent campaign through Alabama and Georgia, all of which were without parallel in our war.

Though these movements constitute one of the most brilliant chapters in our war history,—in fact, in the history of cavalry in any war,—the country really knows little about

them, because they were performed
out of sight in Alabama and Georgia,
while the attention of the country was
fixed upon the fall of Richmond and
the great events immediately follow-
ing it. For this reason it is believed
that the brief story here presented
will not be without interest.

H. V. B.

WASHINGTON, D. C., *September*, 1896.

.

WAS GENERAL THOMAS SLOW AT NASHVILLE?

A NEW generation has come upon the stage since our civil war. It has its own writers on the events of that struggle. Some of these, careful students as they are, make proper and effective use of the stores of material which the Government has collected and published. Others, stumbling upon interesting dispatches of notable campaigns, read them in connection with the ill-considered and hasty criticisms of the hot times which brought them forth, and, finding questions settled twenty years ago, but entirely new to themselves, they proceed to reveal them as new things to the new generation. By this process it has recently been announced that General Thomas was slow at Nashville. To give this echo of thirty-two years ago sufficient voice, several columns of dispatches—which a quarter of a century since formed the basis of discussions that demolished the theory they are now brought forward to sustain—are gravely presented as something new.

Nothing better illustrates this situation than the very familiar story of the Irishman who assaulted the Jew for the part he took in the Crucifixion, and upon being remonstrated with upon the ground that the event occurred eighteen hundred years ago, replied that it was nevertheless new to him, as he had only heard of it the day before.

That General Thomas was not slow at Nashville is ancient history. General Grant, who was the first to charge it, was also the first to withdraw the imputation, by declaring in his official report that at the time he had been very impatient over what appeared as unnecessary delay on the part of Thomas, "but his final defeat of Hood was so complete that it will be accepted as a vindication of that distinguished officer's judgment."

The ostensible reason for heralding Thomas as slow—so slow, indeed, as to require his removal and lead to an order for it—was that he insisted upon concentrating his infantry force and remounting his cavalry. Secretary Stanton declared that the delay would be till doomsday if Thomas waited for the latter.

A consideration of this most important, underlying, and controlling factor in General Thomas's preparations brings up one of the most brilliant chapters in our war history, and altogether the most brilliant in the annals of cavalry operations.

In touching upon General Thomas's

persistence in getting his cavalry ready, it would be very natural for a surface student to quote Secretary Stanton: "If he waits for Wilson to get ready, Gabriel will be blowing his last horn," and treat it as conclusive proof of Thomas's dilatoriness and Stanton's final opinion. But just far enough under the surface to escape the eyes of historical amateurs, lies the splendid and unparalleled fact that in eight winter days after the date of that dispatch General James H. Wilson, Thomas's chief of cavalry, had impressed horses enough, with those furnished on previous requisitions, to raise the effective mounted force at Nashville from 5500 to 13,500, and that on the eighth day General Wilson went into action with 12,000 mounted men, and had besides one brigade of 1500 men engaged in an independent movement.

At this point a moment's considera- tion of the real reasons which caused the outbreak against General Thomas, on the ground that he was slow, will not be out of place.   At City Point it was the perfectly natural but sicken- ing anxiety lest it should turn out that a great mistake had been made in let- ting Sherman march away to the sea, thus possibly opening the way for Hood to the Ohio.   At Savannah it was the same fear, intensified by the consciousness that Thomas had been left with unprepared forces to con- tend against a veteran army which had stubbornly resisted both Thomas and Sherman during the hundred days from Dalton to Atlanta.

And so, while Thomas, as all who were on the ground knew, was making superhuman exertions to prepare fully for the task in hand, he was advised to fight, pressed to fight, ordered to fight, threatened with removal if he did not fight, and his successor dispatched to relieve him. And the underlying cause of it all was the demoralizing fear that Hood might elude or overthrow Thomas and strike for the Ohio, and the country rise in wrath to inquire why Sherman, with 62,000 thoroughly equipped veterans, including a larger force of mounted men than he left behind, had been allowed to march away from the central theater of war. So great was this fear at Savannah that even after receiving Thomas's dispatch giving an account of the first day's battle at Nashville, which resulted in driving Hood's left eight miles (which movement General Grant character-ized as a "splendid success"), Sher-man telegraphed that this attack on Hood "was successful but not com-plete": that he awaited further ac-counts "with anxiety," as Thomas's complete success was necessary to vindicate his own plan for this cam-paign.

Throughout all this inside panic in high official circles, only Thomas and the trusted officers who supported

him at Nashville were cool and un-
moved in the memorable crisis.

THOMAS ORGANIZING HIS ARMY.

The concentration and organization of the fragments which finally
made up the force with which he
practically annihilated his enemy was
one of the most remarkable accom-
plishments of the war. It was prosecuted and consummated in the
immediate presence of the enemy,
and a large portion of the work was
performed during the continued
movement, constant skirmishing, fre-
quent affairs, and one great battle of
an active campaign.

Arriving at Nashville, the first point

of concentration, General Thomas, after careful study of the situation, decided upon his plan of battle. It included, as one of its essentials, the remounting of an effective force of cavalry. From the moment his plans were formed the utmost energy was put forth to prepare for their execution. Greater or more effective activity was never exerted in the Union army than was manifest at Nashville throughout this period. Every stroke of effort was directed toward the predetermined end, with the result which the country knows.

Naturally, the part played by the cavalry in our great battles was often concealed or minimized, while the infantry operations filled the public eye and for the time dimmed the credit due to the cavalry arm. The history of the war does not afford another case where the cavalry formed the determining factor, and, notwithstanding this, where it was so largely overlooked in the distribution of the honors.

It is necessary to a full understanding of the brilliancy, efficiency, and completeness of Thomas's final movements to have in mind the situation after General Sherman had marched away from Hood and left Thomas in Tennessee to stand between that veteran Confederate army and the Ohio.

Preparatory to the march to the sea the great army about Atlanta had been carefully inspected both as to

men and equipments. Every weak
man, all convalescents, those whose
terms of service were expiring—in
short, all the "trash," as General
Sherman expressed it—were sent to
the rear, that is, to Thomas. All
equipments of infantry, artillery, and
cavalry were examined, and every
weak or worn piece replaced by new,
and all the "trash" either destroyed
or "sent to Thomas." The entire
cavalry force was dismounted for
close inspection and for the perfect
remounting of Kilpatrick's column.
Of the sound men whom Thomas received he lost 15,000 by expiration
of terms of service and previous furloughs to vote, within a week after
Hood's movement began.

After this sifting of the armies
General Sherman started for the sea
with 62,000 veterans, of whom he
wrote that "all on this exhibit may
be assumed to have been able-bodied,
experienced soldiers, well armed, well
equipped and provided, so far as
human foresight could, with all the
essentials of life, strength, and vigorous action." With this force was included the entire equipment of trains,
pontoons, and similar essentials which
Thomas, with great care, had per-
fected for the army of the Cumberland. Thomas's request that he
might have his old corps which he
had organized, which had fought
under him so long, was refused, and,
instead, two small corps were sent him.

The nucleus around which General Thomas was to organize an army to take care of Hood—who from May till November had taxed the offensive resources of Sherman's three armies— was, the Fourth Corps, General Stanley, with an effective force of 13,907, and the Twenty-third, General Schofield, with 10,358 effectives.

The means of holding Chattanooga are indicated by the instructions from Sherman to Steedman, whose troops had almost dwindled away by expiration of service: "You must organize and systematize the hospitals and men sent back to Chattanooga. You could use some of them for your forts," and it was suggested to Thomas: "To make things sure, you

might call upon the Governors of
Kentucky and Indiana for some
militia, cautioning them against a
stampede." Thomas was so short of
men that when Steedman asked for
enough for a small but important
garrison, he was obliged to reply:
"You might send a force from the
organization of convalescents now
being made up by General Cruft at
Chattanooga." To which Steedman
replied, "So far, all such detachments reported from the front [Sher-
man] are with furloughs, and are
waiting transportation home."

In place of the 15,000 veterans
whose terms had expired, Thomas
received 12,000 newly enlisted re-
cruits. General A. J. Smith's vet-

eran corps had been ordered from Missouri, and a great parade has been made of this fact by those whose interest it was to show that Thomas had been left with a competent force.   But the fact that it did not arrive at Nashville till after the battle of Franklin, and that Thomas was waiting for it as well as to re-mount the cavalry, was not so loudly proclaimed.

However, when Sherman was ready to start for the sea, with Hood's veteran army concentrated behind him, and Thomas, with the above mentioned elements of an army scat-tered over a territory as large as France, had been assigned to take care of Hood, General Sherman telegraphed Halleck: "I therefore feel no uneasiness as to Tennessee, and have ordered Thomas to assume the offensive in the direction of Selma, Ala." And General Grant, after receiving some inflated figures of a great force left with Thomas, telegraphed Sherman: "With the force you have left with Thomas, he must be able to take care of Hood and destroy him." Later, when the anxiety at City Point referred to in the opening of this paper had become intense, the margin of force with which General Thomas was really operating was found to be so small that General Grant suggested that he should "arm and put in the trenches your quartermaster employees, citizens, etc.," and again, a few hours later, he was suggesting what he could do "with your citizen employees armed."

CONCENTRATING IN FRONT OF HOOD.

It was under such circumstances and conditions which, after all, are but faintly shadowed forth by the facts here stated, that General Thomas began to concentrate his conglomerate forces in Hood's front, and begin under fire the work of organizing and refitting an army. With superhuman effort, and such loyal assistance and energy from officers and soldiers as were not elsewhere exhibited during the war, because not previously required, General Thomas set about the task of preparing the means of overthrowing Hood. Deliberate action and the extreme of prudence were essentials of the situation. The objective of Hood's campaign, under suggestions from President Davis, was the Ohio River. There was no reserve force in sight or within summoning distance, or immediately available anywhere in case of reverses. Thomas could not afford to take the slightest risks so long as his own position was not imperilled. It was not alone the immediate interests confided to his keeping and defense which hinged upon his success or failure, but both Grant and Sherman and possibly the Union itself were to stand or fall with such suc-

cess or failure. Had Hood succeeded, as at the first he might have
succeeded without fault of Thomas,
or even fair ground for reflection
upon him, what would have been said
of Sherman for marching off to the
sea, leaving the central West without
sufficient protection, or of General
Grant for having allowed him to go?

And because the deliberate, pru-
dent, imperturbable, and always successful Thomas appreciated the
situation, and determined to be ready
to annihilate his enemy before he
struck, he was hastily declared to be
slow by those he was preparing to save.

All of General Thomas's troubles
at Nashville arose from his adhering,
in the face of threatened removal, to

plans of action which made General Wilson's cavalry an essential factor in the attack on Hood for which he was energetically preparing. He was looking not only to attack, but to crushing pursuit. In view of the great preponderance of the enemy's cavalry, which was then double his own, and led by Forrest, one of the ablest cavalry generals on either side, effective pursuit without a strong mounted force would be impossible.

The correspondence with Grant— which grew until an order was issued for General Thomas's relief by General Schofield, and, when this was held in abeyance, until a second order for superseding him with General Logan—began with an order from

Grant not to "let Forrest get off without punishment." As Forrest's mounted force was double Wilson's, this was easier to write than to execute. General Thomas therefore explained the situation fully, showing that the cavalry of Hatch and Grierson, which were all the reinforcements he had to depend upon at first, had been turned in at Memphis; that half his own cavalry had been dismounted to equip Kilpatrick's column for Sherman; that his dismounted force, which he had sent to Louisville for horses and arms, was detained there waiting for both, and that as he was greatly outnumbered both in infantry and cavalry he would be compelled to act on the defensive. But he added, in closing:

"The moment I can get my cavalry, I will march against Hood, and if Forrest can be reached he shall be punished."

The day after General Schofield's brilliant and effective battle at Franklin, Thomas made known to Halleck his confidence that Hood could not cross the Cumberland, and therefore thought it best to wait until Wilson could equip his cavalry, as he then felt certain he could whip Hood. Next, the President, through Secretary Stanton, stirred General Grant up by a telegram stating that Mr. Lincoln felt "solicitous about the disposition of Thomas to lay in fortifications for an indefinite period, 'until Wilson gets equipments.'"

THE PANIC AT WASHINGTON.

In spite of the plainest statements of the situation, of the great disparity of forces, of the dictates of prudence to remain on the defensive until he could strike an effective blow, which he expected to deliver in a few days, Thomas was prodded and nagged from City Point and Washington as no officer in command of an army had been before, and treated day by day as if he needed tutelage. In the last dispatch of the series of clear explanations,—which under other circumstances than the seething of that inside panic which a full appreciation of the complications that Sherman's march to the sea had caused would doubtless have been accepted,—General Thomas was peremptorily ordered to "attack Hood at once without waiting for a remount of your cavalry. There is great danger in delay resulting in a campaign back to the Ohio." This was sent in reply to a telegram of Thomas showing that there was the greatest activity in getting the cavalry ready, and he hoped to have it remounted "in three days from this time." To this Thomas replied that he would make all dispositions and attack according to orders, adding, "though I believe it will be hazardous with the small force of cavalry now at my service." Orders to prepare for attack were immediately sent out, and dispositions for the attack began.

Meantime a sleet storm came on which covered the country with a glaze of ice over which neither horses, men, nor artillery could move even on level ground, to say nothing of assaulting an enemy intrenched on the hills. The same day Halleck telegraphed: "If you wait till General Wilson mounts all his cavalry you will wait till doomsday, for the waste equals the supply." And General Grant telegraphed orders relieving Thomas. The latter telegraphed Halleck that he was conscious of having done everything possible to prepare the troops to attack, and if he was removed he would submit without a murmur.

The order of relief was suspended. The sleet storm continued. All of

General Thomas's officers agreed that
it was impracticable to attack. Some
of them even found it impossible to
ride to headquarters because of the
ice, and in the midst of it came an
order from Grant: " I am in hopes of
receiving a dispatch from you to-day
announcing you have moved. Delay no
longer for weather or reinforcements."

Thomas replied :

" I will obey the order as promptly
as possible, however much I regret it,
as the attack will have to be made
under every disadvantage. The whole
country is covered with a perfect sheet
of ice and sleet, and it is with diffi-
culty the troops are able to move
about on level ground."

To Halleck, Thomas replied:

"I have the troops ready to make the attack on the enemy as soon as the sleet which now covers the ground has melted sufficiently to enable the men to march, as the whole country is now covered with a sheet of ice so hard and slippery that it is utterly impossible for troops to ascend the slopes, or even move upon level ground in anything like order. Under these circumstances I believe an attack at this time would only result in a useless sacrifice of life."

The reply to this, unquestionably born of the panic to which allusion has been made, was an order sending General Logan to relieve Thomas. Grant himself then started from City Point for Nashville to assume general command. But the ice having melted, he was met at Washington by the news of Thomas's victory.

The delay that Thomas had insisted upon, in the face of orders twice given for his relief, gave him the cavalry force he required for the decisive blow he intended to strike.

While the official inside at City Point and Washington bordered on panic, everything at Nashville was being pressed forward with activity and vigilance, and at the same time with deliberation, prudence, and the utmost imperturbability. At length, and at the first moment possible consistent with a reasonable expectation of success, the attack began.

THE ATTACK ON HOOD.

The developments of the battle, the energy and success of the pursuit, and the marvelous results of the whole, namely, the virtual destruction of a veteran army, reveal at every step what General Thomas had in mind when he insisted upon waiting till he could remount his cavalry.

In no other battle of the war did cavalry play such a prominent part as in that of Nashville. In no other pursuit did it so distinguish itself. Students of the movement will find themselves constantly questioning, as their investigations proceed, whether, with the force of infantry which General Thomas had been able to

gather, Hood could have been driven
from his position in front of Nashville without the co-operation of the
cavalry. Had Thomas been obliged
to fight without it, as the authorities
at City Point and Washington tried to
compel him to do, it is no reflection
upon his infantry to say that there is
ground for serious doubt as to the result. Hood was intrenched on strong
ground. His positions were commanding. The infantry force against
him was not sufficient in numbers and
experience to make up for the usual
difference due to field works placed as
Hood's were and manned by veterans.
Unquestionably Wilson's cavalry was
the dominating and controlling ele-
ment of the battle. To say this does

447938

not detract from the distinguished infantry generals or their excellent and
brilliant work.   But General Thomas's
plan turned on cavalry work as its
directrix.   His consultations with
General Wilson had been exhaustive.
That officer was charged with re-
organizing, remounting, and refitting
a great cavalry force, even as Thomas
was organizing a new army—under
fire.   There had been nothing like
either of those herculean tasks in any
campaign.

Many officers have organized and
built up an effective cavalry force in
times of rest and peace, but no one
except General Wilson ever did it in
the heat and hurry of a desperate midwinter campaign.   And he could not

have succeeded, nor could any man have accomplished it, in the face of the interferences which were attempted, but for the protection and support of the peerless and imperturbable Thomas.

When General Thomas felt himself to be ready, or so nearly ready that he believed success attainable, he delivered the battle of Nashville. In his whole career he had never struck a blow till he felt himself ready. He looked upon the lives of his soldiers as a sacred trust, not to be carelessly imperiled. Whenever he moved to battle, it was certain that everything had been done that prudence, deliberation, thought, and cool judgment could do under surrounding circum-

stances to insure success commensu-
rate with the cost of the lives of men.
And so it came to pass that when the
war ended it could be truthfully
written of Thomas alone that he never
lost a movement or a battle.

It was an unprecedented array for
attack. The inner lines about the
city were held by quartermasters'
employees. Half the outer, or main
line, was manned mostly by convalescents and new troops; the other, or
right of this line, was occupied by
General A. J. Smith's division. Steedman's provisional division and his two
colored brigades were on the extreme
left of the front, and opened the
battle. The order of infantry in the
line from right to left was Smith's

Corps (Thirteenth), Wood's Corps
(Fourth), Schofield's Corps (Twenty-
third), and Steedman's troops.

THE CAVALRY IN THE BATTLE.

Wilson's cavalry was massed behind
the extreme right. Steedman, on the
left, early December 15, delivered a
vigorous and successful attack. It
was in the nature of a feint. Meantime the grand play with the cavalry
began. Its part was the imposing
swinging movement of 12,000 mounted
men against and around the Confederate left. Before the short, lower-
ing winter day had closed, this force
had overrun several redoubts on the
enemy's left, capturing them and their
artillery by assaults, swept for eight

miles over ground of formidable
natural difficulties, and forced itself
to the immediate flank and rear of
Hood's main line of works. It rode
to its firing lines and fought dismounted.

The enemy's left being thus effect-
ually turned, the infantry attack in
front was delivered with success, and
Hood fell back to a new line, and
early the second day withdrew still
further, establishing his right on the
Overton Hills.

The second day was a repetition of
the first. Wilson again swung his
cavalry by a wide detour to the
enemy's left and rear, and from the
rear assaulted and carried a portion
of his main line, capturing both works

and guns. Thereupon the infantry corps again advanced on the front; the enemy was everywhere forced back in confused retreat, and instantly the most vigorous pursuit began, and was kept up that night till midnight, the cavalry leading. It was resumed at daylight and continued night and day in winter weather,—rain, slush, snow, and ice,—over a soggy country and mud roads which were well-nigh impassable, leading through a region which both armies had gleaned bare with their foraging parties. But even under these conditions, by herculean efforts, the most vigorous pursuit was prosecuted to the Tennessee River. The determined character of this pursuit is well illustrated by the fact that

6000 cavalry horses were disabled, so
rapid and exhaustive was the work
they performed.   At the close Hood's
army was practically destroyed.   It
opened the campaign 55,000 strong.
It lost nearly all its guns and equipments, about 15,000 killed and
wounded, and the same number of
prisoners.   About 13,000 men of all
arms were finally assembled at Tupelo.
Starting toward North Carolina it
continued to disintegrate, and reached
the southern line of that State not
over 6000 strong.   It had practically
disappeared as an army.   When it
reached Bentonville in Sherman's
front it went into action with only
3953 officers and men of all arms.
For the first time in the war one of

the leading veteran armies of the enemy operating in the open field had been destroyed. This was the direct result of Thomas's blow at Nashville, and the pursuit which followed.

Thomas was very deeply pained and indignant at the treatment he received while making the most vigorous preparations for battle which it was possible to carry forward. He called his officers together during the sleet storm to tell them of the peremptory order to attack without regard to weather, and of his reply that the conditions were unfavorable for attack, that it would be made at the first possible moment, and that if removed, as threatened, he would sub-

mit without a murmur. He found
himself fully supported by all of them.
After this meeting was over he called
General Wilson aside and said: ''Wilson, they treat me at Washington and
at Grant's headquarters as though I
were a boy! They do not seem to
think that I have sense enough to plan
a campaign or fight a battle, but if
they will only let me alone a few days
I will show them that they are mis-
taken. I am sure we will whip Hood
and destroy his army, if we go at them
under favorable instead of unfavorable
conditions.''

Later, and in spite of his brilliant
and complete victory, and the further
fact that such vigorous pursuit as had
never before been made by a Union

army was in progress, in midwinter and under more unfavorable circumstances, too, than a pursuing army had encountered during the war, this nagging from Washington and City Point continued.

Secretary Stanton alone was immediate, wholesouled, and continuing in his congratulations and praises. Grant tempered his message over the "splendid success" with the information that he had reached Washington on his way to relieve him, but now would not proceed, and continued: "Push the enemy now and give him no rest until he is entirely destroyed. Much is now expected." Mr. Lincoln added to his thanks: "You made a magnificent beginning.

A grand consummation is within your easy reach.   Do not let it slip."

In the midst of these proddings, Secretary Stanton suggested to Grant that Thomas be made a Major-General.   Grant replied: " I think Thomas has won the Major-Generalcy, but I would wait a few days before giving it, to see the extent of damage done."

Next came Halleck, in the midst of the almost superhuman efforts of the pursuit:

" Permit me, General, to urge the vast importance of a hot pursuit of Hood's army.   Every possible sacrifice should be made, and your men for a few days will submit to any hardship and privation to accomplish the great result. A most vigorous pursuit on your part is therefore of vital importance to Sherman's plans. No sacrifice must be spared to attain so important an object."

THOMAS TURNS ON HIS NAGGERS.

There was one thing in which General Thomas was slow. He was not swift to give expression to indignation over wrong treatment. To this latter, as the culmination of the series, he at last responded with this crushing statement:

" General Hood's army is being pursued as rapidly and as vigorously as it is possible for one army to pursue another. We cannot control the elements, and you must remember that to resist Hood's advance into Tennessee I had to reorganize and almost thoroughly equip the force now under my command. I fought the battles of the 15th and 16th inst. with the troops but partially equipped, and notwithstanding the inclemency of the weather and the partial equipment, have been enabled to drive the enemy beyond Duck River, crossing the two streams with my troops, and driving the enemy from position to position, without the aid of pontoons, and with but little transportation to bring up supplies and ammunition.

"I am doing all in my power to crush Hood's army, and, if it be possible, will destroy it, but pursuing an enemy through an exhausted country,

over mud roads, completely sogged
with heavy rains, is no child's play,
and cannot be accomplished as quickly
as thought of.   I hope, in urging me
to push the enemy, the department
remembers that General Sherman took
with him the complete organizations
of the Military Division of the Mississippi, well equipped in every respect
as regards ammunition, supplies, and
transportation, leaving me only two
corps—partially stripped of their transportation to accommodate the force
taken with him—to oppose the advance
into Tennessee of that army which
had resisted the advance of the army
of the Military Division of the Mississippi on Atlanta from the com-
mencement of the campaign until its

close, and which is now, in addition, aided by Forrest's cavalry. Although my progress may appear slow, I feel assured that Hood's army can be driven from Tennessee, and eventually driven to the wall, by the force under my command, but too much must not be expected of troops which have to be reorganized, especially when they have the task of destroying a force in a winter campaign which was able to make an obstinate resistance to twice its numbers in spring and summer. In conclusion, I can safely state that this army is willing to submit to any sacrifice to oust Hood's army, or to strike any other blow which would contribute to the destruction of the rebellion."

The next day Stanton thus again extended his steady support:

"I have seen to-day General Halleck's dispatch of yesterday and your reply. It is proper for me to assure you that this department has the most unbounded confidence in your skill, vigor, and determination to employ to the best advantage all the means in your power to pursue and destroy the enemy. No department could be inspired with more profound admiration and thankfulness for the great deeds you have already performed, or more confiding faith that human effort could accomplish no more than will be done by you and the gallant officers and soldiers of your command."

To this Thomas responded in terms which show his deep appreciation of the only unqualifiedly friendly voice that had reached his ear from those in high authority:

"I am profoundly thankful for the hearty expression of your confidence in my determination and desire to do all in my power to destroy the enemy and put down the rebellion."

As pertinent to this history it is well to recall two facts: First, Sherman reached Savannah, having avoided all fortified places, had encountered no enemy in force during his march, sat down before the city, and awoke one morning to find that Hardee with his 10,000 men had slipped out of the city over the river and escaped.

Second, the Army of the Potomac, which had 87,000 present for duty equipped, and which was not obliged to depend upon quartermasters' employees, citizens, and convalescents for its reserves, remained quietly in its camps in front of City Point and in sight of the enemy from November to April, giving plenty of leisure for complaining that the Army of the Cumberland did not attack at the dropping of a handkerchief.

With the dispersion of Hood's army General Thomas set about preparing for a spring campaign which should open at the earliest possible day. His plan contemplated the assembling and putting in thorough condition an army of cavalry to penetrate the

South under his trusted commander, General James H. Wilson.

THE CAVALRY AFTER NASHVILLE.

Six divisions of the cavalry corps were put in camp, extending for twelve miles along the north bank of the Tennessee from Gravelly Springs to Waterloo Landing. A winter campaign was laid out at army headquarters for Thomas's army, to begin without rest or refitting—the resting to be done by proxy in the vicinity of City Point. But owing to rains and unusual floods this plan for Thomas could not be pursued, and the time was improved for a vigorous and rapid refitting of his forces.

Early in March a cavalry corps of

27,000 had been gathered. The men were veterans. The new equipment collected was excellent, but, with all that the Cavalry Bureau could do, only 17,000 horses could be provided. This force was raised, by drills and every form of perfecting an organization, to a high state of efficiency. While vigorous efforts were in progress to equip Hatch's veteran division of 10,000, the orders from Washington and City Point for forward movement began to pour in on Thomas. While no other national army was moving, the nine weeks of midwinter which Thomas was using in most active measures for beginning a crushing campaign were begrudged him, and he was again prodded to move before he was ready. Next, the breaking up of the cavalry force which had been assembled and prepared with such great labor began. One division, 5000 strong, was ordered off to Canby at Mobile, where its operations proved of little consequence, and Thomas was ordered with 5000 more to make a demonstration on Tuscaloosa and Selma.

General Wilson then urged with great ability and power that the cavalry should go as a body, with the purpose of destroying the various factories of war material and breaking the interior lines of communication and supply. Grant, who had great confidence in Wilson from his long service on his staff, consented, and the plan, warmly approved by Thomas, was adopted, and Wilson was started with all the powers of an independent commander.

On the 22d of March Wilson had crossed the Tennessee and started toward Selma. He had three divisions, Upton's, Long's, and E. M. McCook's. The aggregate strength was 12,500 mounted, and 1500 dismounted to follow till they could be furnished with captured horses. It was in every sense a command thoroughly equipped and fully supplied. The divisions marched on different roads, but the objective of each was Selma. The direct distance was 180 miles, and the average march of each division to reach it was 250 miles. The streams were still flooded in all directions, and the roads deep and difficult. The vigor and skill with which all these obstacles were overcome form a brilliant chapter, not exceeded in kind during the war.

At Montevallo, forty-five miles from Selma, a portion of Forrest's command was encountered, and, after a dashing fight, forced to retreat. The Southern leader had not been able, as yet, to concentrate his command. The capture of a courier with dispatches to Forrest showed Wilson how several columns were moving to join Forrest, and forces were sent in various directions to check them, while Wilson's main column rode direct for Selma. It was an exciting

and successful play. Forrest, when
reached, was found to have made the
best disposition possible for an in-
ferior force, and maintained a stubborn resistance. But the Union
troopers charged at all points. Forrest himself fought hand to hand,
and received several saber strokes.
After the lines were carried Wilson's
column advanced in pursuit twenty-
five miles, and bivouacked at night
only twenty miles from Selma.

Selma contained a gun foundry,
arsenal, and important manufactories
of war material. The place had been
sufficiently fortified, as was believed,
against any possible cavalry attack.
General Wilson had succeeded in ob-
taining accurate plans of these works

and of the grounds in front of them. During the day's advance, which was not retarded by Forrest, these sketches were shown to all general officers and a plan of attack explained. As a result, upon reaching the vicinity of the works, the various brigades went into position with precision and celerity, and the storming of the intrenchments began at once. Just as darkness was gathering they were carried at every point. The resistance was stubborn, but numbers, efficient organization, equipment, and dash won the day and the city.

The capture of Selma was one of the most remarkable feats in the cavalry annals of any land. The works contained 24 bastions and a number of strong redans with deep ditches, while the curtains of the four-mile line were generally stockaded rifle pits. There was besides an interior line of 4 detached forts. The artillery armament of these works was 30 field guns and two thirty-pounder Parrotts. Wilson's attacking force was 8000. Forrest, for the defense, had half that force of veteran cavalry, and some 2000 militia, home-guards, and citizens. The captures were 2700 prisoners, nearly 2000 horses, 32 guns in service, 26 field guns mounted complete in arsenal, 46 siege guns in the foundry, 66,000 rounds of artillery ammunition, and 100,000 rounds for small arms. General Wilson destroyed the Selma arsenal, with 44 buildings covering 13 acres, filled with machinery and munitions; powder works comprising 7 buildings, with 14,000 pounds of powder; niter works, with 18 buildings equipped, 3 gun foundries, 3 rolling mills, and several machine shops, all equipped and turning out material of war, and vast accumulations of quartermaster and commissary stores. It was a crushing blow to the Confederacy—this capture of Selma with its enormous military plant on Sunday, April 2. The same day Grant, at the other end of the line a thousand miles away, had broken the lines at Petersburg, and the evacuation of Richmond began.

THE CAPTURE OF MONTGOMERY.

General Wilson's command remained at Selma about a week, making active preparations for its next stroke, which was to be against Montgomery, the former capital of the Confederacy. It was necessary to prepare a thousand feet of bridging to cross the Alabama River, then at flood tide and filled with floating *débris.* Equipments of every kind were looked after and the most careful refitting of the whole command took place, the Confederate stores taken offering abundant facilities for such important work. There had been horses enough captured to mount the whole command, together with a very considerable force of negroes for fatigue purposes. With Croxton's brigade detached and moving by a circuitous route from central Alabama, through northern Georgia toward Macon, the final objective, the force of the main column was reduced to 11,000 men.

Upon reaching the outskirts of Montgomery they were met by the officials of the town and leading citizens, offering surrender without conditions. Then followed an astonishment for the people of this capital. The whole force, marching in close column, with its flags unfurled and music playing, made its way into and through the city without a marauder leaving its column or a soldier entering a private house in any quarter uninvited. And, so far as information came to the officers of the command, not an insulting word was spoken. The main portion of the command camped in the vicinity of the city, while its advance continued rapidly toward Columbus, skirmishing with the retreating enemy. There was a very considerable capture of steamboats loaded with military supplies at Montgomery. The halt there, however, was only for the night, and the next day the main column moved with the greatest celerity so as to secure a bridge for crossing the Chattahoochee either at Columbus on the direct road to Macon, or at West Point, further up the river.

By rapid movements, and bold and most brilliant fighting, both the bridge at Columbus and that at West Point were captured. Though both were prepared for burning and protected by heavy fortifications well manned by a defending force, the attacks against these were pushed so vigorously as to make it impossible for the enemy to fire them.

The bridge-head at West Point was protected by a strong redoubt with a deep ditch mounting two guns, one a thirty-two pounder, and the work manned by 265 men. This was twice attacked by direct assault, and carried the second time. The captures were 3 guns, 500 stands of small arms, 19 locomotive engines, and 240 cars loaded with army supplies, but the greatest importance of securing a crossing at West Point was that it opened a way direct to Macon, which could be used for the entire cavalry corps in case the attack at Columbus should fail.

The main column arrived at Girard, a small town opposite Columbus, early in the afternoon, finding a heavy line of fortifications protecting three bridges across the Chattahoochee. Under a vigorous attack upon the lower bridge the Confederates found it impossible to save it from capture unless it was destroyed, and set fire to the cotton and turpentine with which it had been prepared for burning.

It was then decided to make a night attack upon the central bridge, and the troops were arranged for this desperate work. The lines were very quietly formed, and moved up to within range of the intrenchments, and at a signal the assault began. The works were found to be strong and thoroughly protected with ditches and slashed timber. The enemy, while watchful, was not expecting a night assault from troops that had not reconnoitered the fortifications by daylight. They opened fire upon the charging columns, but in the darkness it was necessarily wild and uncertain.

The Union troops went over the works at many points, and all rushed in haste toward the bridge, which was the objective point of the attack. It

was one of the most desperate and
persistent night fights of the war, but
so thoroughly organized was the attacking force that in spite of the darkness and confusion it was able to
move with sufficient unity to preserve
its columns and formations. Upon
the penetration of the works both
Union and Confederate soldiers swept
over the bridge toward Columbus,
and this was so crowded with the men
of both forces that the enemy holding the works at the east end of the
bridge, and commanding it with artillery, were restrained from firing till
the Union forces made a rush upon
them and gained possession, and
Columbus was in full possession of
General Wilson's forces.

The next morning it was ascertained that the works had been manned and defended by 3000 Georgia militia under Generals Howell Cobb and Toombs. The capture of the city resulted in the destruction of a great quantity of war material, over 60 guns, the ram *Jackson*, mounting 6 guns, a large number of small arms, 125,000 bales of cotton, 15 locomotives, 250 cars, a navy yard and armory, 2 rolling mills, 1 arsenal and nitre works, 2 powder magazines, 2 iron works, 3 foundries, 10 mills and factories turning out war material, 100,000 rounds of artillery ammunition, and a great quantity of machinery used in the manufacture of war material.

THE CAVALRY AT COLUMBUS.

Columbus was the great manufacturing center of the Confederacy, and this destruction inflicted irreparable damage. While little was known at the North of this sweep of Wilson's columns through the industrial centers and military storehouses of the Confederacy, it is easy to understand that these fatal blows at vital points of interior military supply added to the demoralization and discouragement attending the evacuation of Richmond and the gathering storm about the armies of Lee and Johnson.

The column moved swiftly for Macon, and about eighteen miles out from it the officer in advance

was met with a flag of truce carry-
ing a note from General Beauregard notifying the commander of
the forces of General Sherman's
truce with General Johnston, stating
that an agreement had been entered
upon that the contending forces were
to occupy their present positions till
forty-eight hours' notice had been
given of the resumption of hostilities.
As General Wilson was eight or ten
miles in the rear with his main command, the note was sent to him, and
the officer in the advance pushed to and
into Macon, taking possession of the
city. When General Wilson arrived in
the city he went at once to the city hall,
where Generals Howell Cobb, Gus-
tavus W. Smith, and others had been

confined. General Cobb demanded
that he and his command should be
released, and that General Wilson
should retire to where the flag of
truce had met his advance. General
Wilson declared that after receiving
the note he had lost no time in push-
ing on to the head of his column, and
found it in full possession of the city.
He could not accept notification of a
truce through the Confederate authorities, as they were not his channel of
communication with General Sherman, and ended the conference by a
positive refusal to acknowledge the
armistice, to retire from the town, or
to release his prisoners. When he
announced this decision he said to
General Cobb that he could conceive

of but one adequate reason for the truce, and that was that Lee's army had surrendered. Cobb, however, declined to give any information, but General Smith, to whom Wilson addressed the same remark, answered that Lee had surrendered, and that peace would soon follow. Thereupon General Wilson announced his decision to remain at Macon and conduct his future operations upon the principle that every man killed thereafter was a man murdered.

This interview was held on the 20th of April just before midnight, and was the first definite knowledge which Wilson's column had obtained of the events which had occurred in Virginia.

The surrender at Macon included

a large number of small guns and a great quantity of military stores and supplies. The next day the Confederate authorities opened communication over their own telegraph lines between Wilson and Sherman, and the former received orders from the latter to desist from hostilities pending an armistice. Soon after he received orders from the Secretary of War, through Thomas, to disregard this armistice and resume operations, but before this order reached him he learned that Johnston had surrendered all the Confederate forces east of the Mississippi, and that peace was assured.

The closing act of General Wilson's campaign was the capture of Jefferson

Davis by regiments from his command. Thus ended the most noted cavalry movement of the war.

The above is of necessity a very concise presentation of the salient points of General Wilson's remarkable campaign, conducted alone by mounted troops. It is not claimed that the account is new. I have published it heretofore in extended form, though not in the press. This briefer story cannot but be a repetition of the facts and a synopsis of the fuller statement of them. It is a chapter in our war history than which no other is more replete with thrilling and brilliant incident, with skillful planning, and bold and successful execution. No purely cavalry campaign

in our war approached it in these
features. It is doubtful whether its
parallel can be found in the cavalry
annals of any modern nation. And to
this general statement should be added
that the officer who commanded it,
who was its organizer and its controlling spirit, the one upon whom
General George H. Thomas leaned as
one of his most trusted lieutenants
and advisers, was only twenty-seven
years old.

It is not strange that Lee's and
Johnston's surrender fixed the attention of the country and turned it
away from General Wilson's campaign.
Had these two events been delayed a
month the land would have rung with
Wilson's praises and with new honors

for General Thomas. Indeed, had
the withdrawal from Richmond and
the events which so quickly followed
it been only delayed in their beginning by a few days necessary to have
informed the country of Wilson's marvelous successes, it is certain that his
breaking up of these interior storehouses of military material, and the
destruction of these many plants for
producing more, would have insepa-
rably and largely connected themselves in the minds of the people with
the eastern surrender as cause and
effect.

It was a campaign whose success
would have been the same had Lee
been able to hold on to Richmond,
and had Johnston so eluded Sherman

as to prolong the contest in Virginia and North Carolina.

THOMAS'S PLAN THOUGHT OUT AND FOLLOWED.

From the first this cavalry campaign had proceeded according to a clearly formed plan. It was made after full conference with General Wilson. First, it was decided that to render an attack upon Hood's line certain of success a sufficient cavalry force must be in hand to turn his flank. The next requirement, that of pursuing so effectively as to break up Hood, could not be met without sufficient cavalry. So General Thomas held on in the face of what has been related till he was so nearly ready to strike that he felt certain of success. As a result, the ends in view were attained. The cavalry flanking circuits made possible the driving of the enemy from his extended position. The pursuit by a thoroughly equipped cavalry force made possible and secured the virtual destruction of Hood's army.

The next campaign, urged by Wilson and approved by Thomas, had for its objective the destruction of the military storehouses and manufactories, and the fatal crippling of the Confederacy. How complete was the success of this second campaign the outlines already presented sufficiently attest.

In summarizing this attempt to

again direct attention to this wonderful cavalry campaign, it may be permissible to repeat the form in which I have heretofore set it forth in a volume (the concluding chapters of Colonel Donn Piatt's "Life of Thomas") covering the ground of this article at much greater length:

It should be remembered forever in the annals of war that Thomas insisted upon waiting to remount a portion of the (cavalry) corps before he would consent to deliver battle, and that when he did march forth against the veteran and almost invincible infantry of Hood, strongly intrenched in his front, it was the cavalry corps which broke through his left, and wheeling grandly in the same direction, captured twenty-seven guns from their redoubts on the first day, and which, continuing its movement on the second day, enveloped and took in reverse the left and left center of the Confederate intrenchments, and so shook their entire line as to make it a walkover for the infantry which Thomas finally hurled against them. It was the harrassing pursuit of Hood by the cavalry corps which, notwithstanding the rains and sleet of midwinter and the swollen rivers, broke up and scattered the host which had so confidently invaded Middle Tennessee only a month before. Pausing on the banks of the Tennessee till the rough edge of winter had passed, to gather in the distant detachments, to

procure remounts, clothing, and equipments, and to weld the growing force
into a compact and irresistible army
corps of horsemen, the cavalry commander, with the full concurrence of
Thomas, the beau ideal of American
soldiers, began his final and most glori-
ous campaign. No historian or military critic can read the story of the
operations which followed without
coming to the conclusion that they
were characterized by the most remarkable series of successes ever
gained by cavalry in modern warfare.
They illustrate, first, the importance
of concentrating that arm in compact
masses under one competent commander, and in operations of the first
importance; second, the tremendous

advantage of celerity of movement, especially in modern warfare, where improved firearms play such a decisive part; third, that the chief use of horses, notwithstanding that they may in exceptional cases add to the shock of the charge, is to transport fighting men rapidly to the vital point of a battlefield, and especially to the flank and rear of the enemy's position, or deeply into the interior of the enemy's country against his lines of supply and communication, and also his arsenals, armories, and factories; fourth, that the best infantry armed with the best magazine carbines or rifles make the best mounted troops, irrespective of whether they be called cavalry, dragoons, or mounted infantry.

When the fact is recalled that the seven divisions of this corps at the close of the war mustered about 35,000 men for duty with the colors, and that had the war lasted sixty days longer they could, and probably would, have been concentrated in Virginia, it will be seen to what a high degree of perfection the organization had been brought, and that it fully justified Sherman's declaration that it was by far the largest, most efficient, and most powerful body of horse that had ever come under his command. But when the captures of the strongly fortified towns of Selma, West Point, and Columbus are considered, with all the romantic incidents of night fighting, together with

the surrender of the no less strongly
fortified cities and towns of Montgomery, Macon, and West Point, car-
rying with them the destruction of the
last and only remaining arsenals,
armories, factories, storehouses, and
military munitions and supplies, and
also the destruction of the railways
connecting those places with their
bridges and rolling stock, it will be
seen that Johnston and his generals
had nothing else left them but to
lay down their arms and surrender.
It was no longer possible for them
to concentrate an army, or to supply it with food, or to keep it armed
and equipped.   With those places
and the manufacturing plants which
they contained still in their pos-

session, and with the railways connecting them still unbroken, they
might have collected together in the
Carolinas a force amply able to cope
with Sherman, and possibly to over-
whelm him before reinforcements
could reach him. That brilliant but
erratic leader, with his splendid army,
it will be remembered, had avoided
Macon on the one hand and Augusta
on the other, both the seats of important military industries, and by an
eccentric and unnecessary movement
from his true line of operations, had
gone to Savannah, leaving the direct
railroads and highways behind him
open and free for the use of the rem-
nants of Hood's army and of the
other scattered detachments which

were hastening to form a junction with Johnston, now the sole hope of the Confederacy.

Had it not been for Wilson's wide swath of victory and destruction through and not around the important cities in his way, during which he captured 8500 prisoners and 280 guns, and afterward paroled 59,000 rebel soldiers belonging to the armies of Lee, Johnston, and Beauregard, it would have been easy for Johnston and Beauregard, had they been so minded, to continue the war indefinitely. As it was, to continue it was simply impossible, and for this the country is indebted, first, to Wilson and his gallant troopers, and second, to Thomas, who insisted

that they should have time to remount and prepare for the work before them. Neither the army nor the
country ever appreciated that invincible body of horsemen, or their division, brigade, regimental, and company
commanders, or the high character of
the enlisted men, or the performances
of the whole at their real worth.
There were officers among them fit
for any command that could have been
given them, and as a body they were
as gallant and capable soldiers as ever
drew saber or wore uniform. Had
the war lasted a few months longer
their fame would have been a house-
hold word. The leaders, though
young in years, were old in war.
Wilson himself was at the close not

yet twenty-eight. Kilpatrick was about the same age. Upton was several months younger. Winslow, Alexander, Croxton, La Grange, Watkins, Atkins, Murray, Palmer, Noble, Kitchell, Benteen, Cooper, Young, Bacon, and Weston were of the younger set, while McCook, Minty, Long, Hatch, R. W. Johnson, Knipe, Kelly, Hammond, Coon, G. M. L. Johnson, Spalding, Pritchard, Miller, Harrison, Biggs, Vail, Israel Garrard, McCormick, Pierce, and Frank White were somewhat older, though none of them had reached middle life. Harnden, as sturdy as Balfour of Burleigh, and Eggleston, the type of those who rode with Cromwell at Marston Moor, were graybeards, but were full of activity and courage. Ross Hill and Taylor, although captains, were mere boys, but full of experienced valor.

The men in the ranks were mostly from the Western and Northwestern and upper slave States, and of them it may be truthfully averred that their superiors for endurance, self-reliance, and pluck could nowhere be found. After they were massed at Nashville they believed themselves to be invincible, and it was their boast that they had never come in sight of a hostile gun or fortification that they did not capture. Armed with Spencers, it was their conviction that elbow to elbow, dismounted, in single line, nothing could withstand their charge. "Only cover our flanks," said Miller to Wilson, as they were approaching Selma, "and nothing can stop us !" In conclusion, it may be safely said that no man ever saw one of them in the closing campaign of the war skulking before battle or sneaking to the rear after the action began. They seemed to know by instinct when and where the enemy might be encountered, and then the only strife among them was to see who should be first in the onset. With a corps of such men, properly mounted and armed, and with such organization and discipline as prevailed among them during their last great campaign, no hazard of war can be regarded as too great for them to undertake, and nothing should be counted as impossible except defeat.

When the "records" are all published and the story properly written, it will show that no corps in the army, whether cavalry or infantry, ever inflicted greater injury upon the "Lost Cause," or did more useful service toward the re-establishment of the Union under the Constitution and the laws, than was done by the cavalry corps of the Military Division of the Mississippi.

THE END.

www.ingramcontent.com/pod-product-compliance
Lightning Source LLC
Chambersburg PA
CBHW021413090426
42742CB00009B/1123